The BROONS

D.C. THOMSON & Co. Ltd., GLASGOW: LONDON: DUNDEE

£1.60

The BROONS

The Broons have never had a pet
Like other families do.
Maw says if they a' had their pick
The place would be a zoo!

But just suppose they had their choice,
What would their wee pet be?
They've a' got different thoughts on it,
So let's peep in an' see . . .

A talking bird is Daphne's choice,
It s voice her heart would thrill.
She'd teach it to say clever things,
Like, " Who's a pretty girl?"

Hen pines for something quite unique—
A fine, lang-legged cuddy.
" But why lang legs?" you well may ask—
Tae stop his feet gettin' muddy!

Now Paw dreams o' a handy pet—
It's nothing wi' fins or flippers.
A' he fancies is a couthie wee dug
Tae fetch his pipe an' slippers!

The Twins plump for an elephant,
Tae perform a special trick.
Each time they pass an aipple tree,
Jings, they could hae their pick!

When Horace canna dae his sums,
Ye'll never see him madder.
His choice o' pet would be a snake—
A special one—an Adder!

But Maw just smiles at a' their dreams—
She's got her ain wee pet!
And, aye, they a' agree the Bairn's
The bonniest " wee lamb " yet!

Printed and published by D. C. Thomson & Co., Ltd., 185 Fleet Street, London EC4A 2HS.
© D. C. Thomson & Co., Ltd., 1983.
ISBN 0 85116 294 0

It's hard luck for Paw Broon—

When the snow tumbles doon!

The Broons are up to ninety-nine—

But good auld Gran'paw's doin' fine!

Maggie's bein' an awfy bore—

But, jings, she's got a shock in store!

A quiet night withoot TV—

But still they canna a' agree!

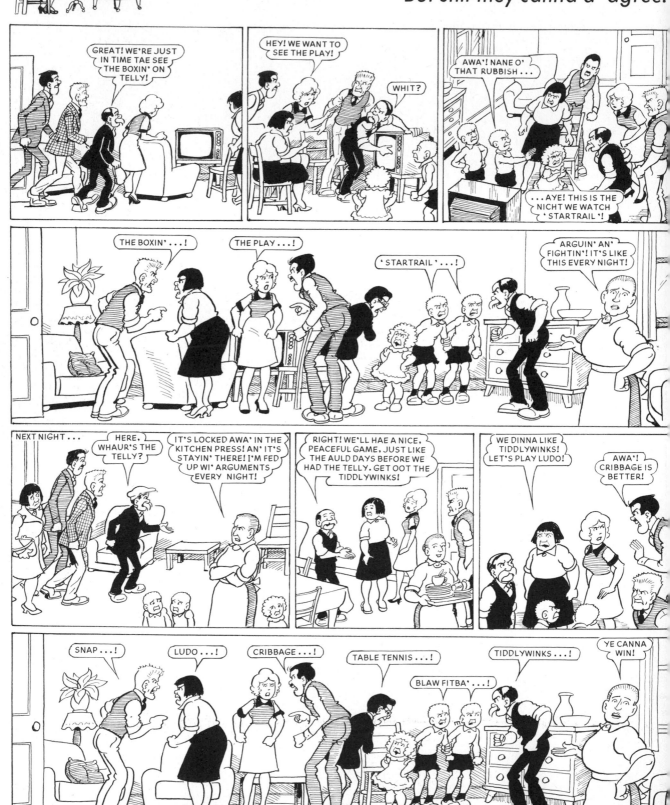

Well, well, well—

What tales they tell!

. . . but there's a catch—

At this fitba match!

Nae wonder Paw Broon's lang in the mooth—

He hasna got a single tooth!

Sew this, stitch that, stitch that, sew this—

But they a' know what day it is!

This smart daughter—

Lands her Paw in " hot water "!

COME AND SEE THE HOOSE DAVE IS THINKING OF BUYING ON THE NEW ESTATE.

AT THE HOUSE—

OF COURSE, IT HAS CENTRAL HEATING!

BUT HE'LL NO' HAE A MANTELPIECE TAE PIT HIS FEET ON!

THEN HERE WE HAVE THE BUILT-IN WARDROBES!

THEY'RE NAE GUID! YE'VE NAE TOP TAE PUT YOUR JUNK ON!

THE COOKER HAS AN EXTRACTOR FAN ABOVE IT TO TAKE AWAY THE COOKING SMELLS.

DAFT! THERE'S NOTHING BETTER THAN THE SMELL O' HOME-MADE BROTH!

THERE'S A SHOWER HERE INSTEAD OF A BATH. OF COURSE, YOU'LL NOT LIKE THAT, PAW.

EH? WHY NO'?

BECAUSE YOU WOULDN'T BE ABLE TO PLAY WITH THE BAIRN'S TOY BOATS AND RUBBER DUCKS, LIKE YOU DO AT HOME!

Ooh, the pain—

When Paw's caught in the rain!

Here's a laugh for you—

A one-man queue!

Help m'boab! Michty me!—

Here's a real CATastrophe

The lassies winna live it doon—

If they've upset auld Gran'paw Broon!

" Never a borrower or lender be!"

Who says that? Just look and see

The meal Maw cooks—

Brings funny looks!

"Scrub the stairs?" says Paw. "Awa'!"—

But here's a sight tae please poor Maw!

There's a " brush-off " in store—

For this bloke at the door!

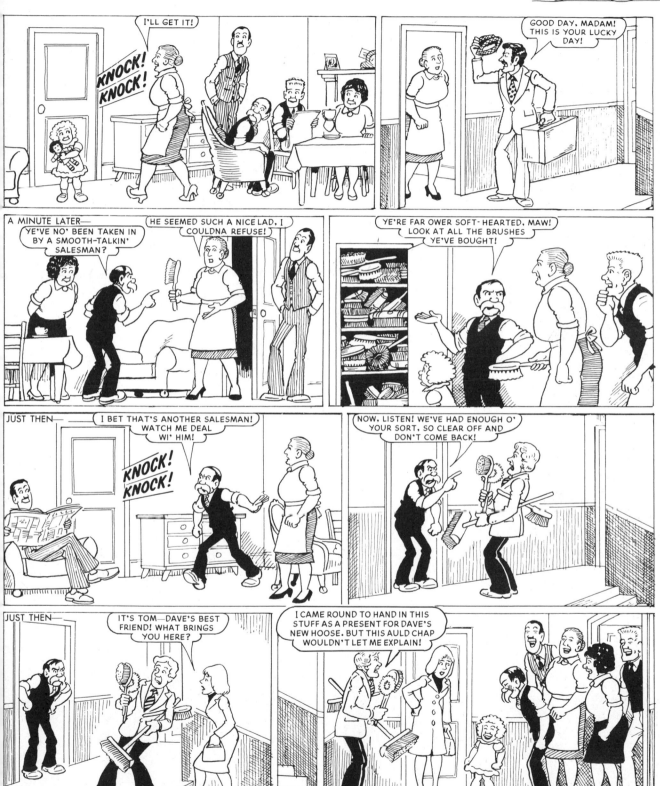

An expert cook?—

Well, tak' a look!

They're up to high doh when—

It's music time at No. 10

It disnae go far—

but it's a smashing car!

Things dinna go tae plan—

Wi' this fancy caravan!

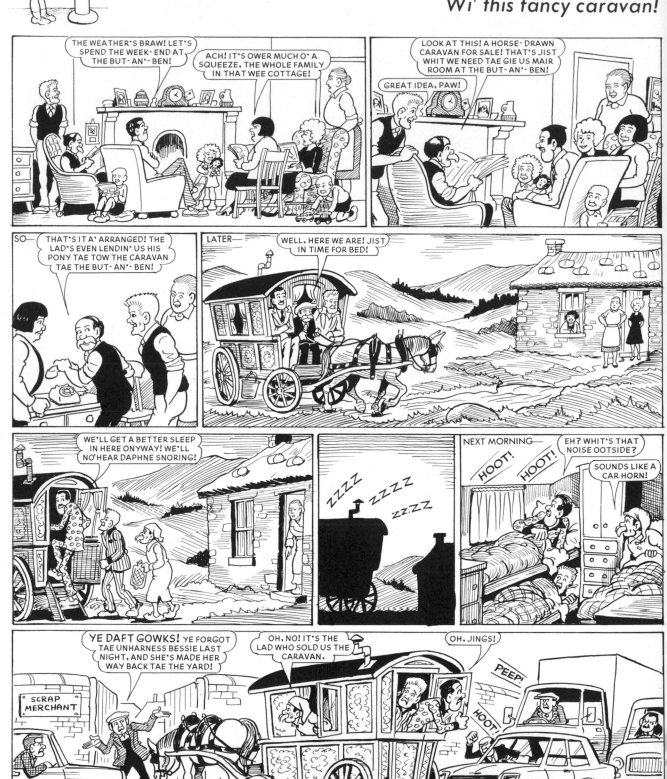

This " antique " shopper—

Comes a cropper!

It seems the Broons just canna win—

Wherever they go, there's lots o' din!

Joe Broon's amazed tae see—

The folk who come tae tea!

The family chuckle when they find—

Why the Bairn lags behind!

Well, did ye ever!—

Paw's " bin " too clever!

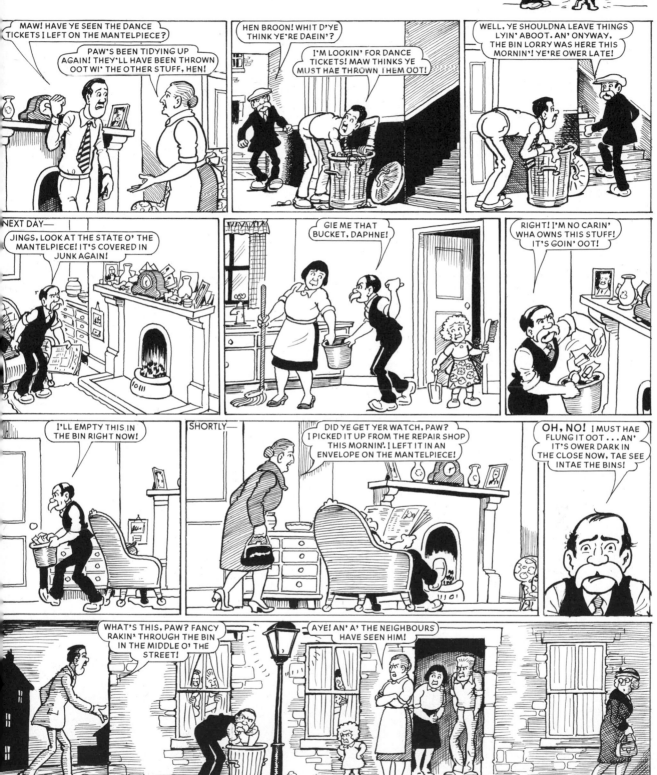

It's a real laughalot—

When they see what Paw's bough

it the women or is it the men—

Who wear the breeks at No. 10?

They're a' surprised at Gran'paw's plan—

Tae add a grannie tae the clan

That angry fist comes thumpin' doon—

Then things look black for puir Paw Broon!

A slip-up by Paw—

Means " feet-up " for Maw!

Here's a real laughalot—

Wi' the ring Alfie bought!

This ploy starts off with Joe and Hen—

Aye, just the twa o' them—and then . . .

There's a funny sight standin'—

On the Broons' landin'!

Electric shocks—

Then troublesome locks!

Now here's a funny hobby—

Reading in the lobby!

No wonder Paw's grumpy—

His porridge is lumpy!

Half a pie, half a paper—
This day's no' half a proper caper!

DIGGING GRAN'PAW'S GARDEN TOOK LONGER THAN WE THOUGHT, JOE. WE'VE MISSED HALF THE MATCH!

AYE! AN' WE'VE HAD NO' DENNER. STILL, WE CAN GET A PIE INSIDE.

BUT— SORRY, LADS! YE'RE OWER LATE! I'VE ONLY ONE PIE LEFT.

REFRESHMENTS
TEAS—SANDWICHES—PIES

HUH! ONLY HALF A PIE AN' HALF A MATCH!

AFTER THE GAME—
HERE'S THE EARLY SPORTS EDITION. WE'LL SEE WHIT WE MISSED IN THE FIRST HALF.

THAT SOUNDS LIKE A BRAW GOAL BY UNITED WE MISSED!

BUS STOP

HOI! WATCH OOT! SORRY, MISTER!

BUS STOP

NOW WE'VE GOT HALF A PAPER!

WHIT A DAY WE'VE HAD, MAW!

WELL, YE'RE JIST IN TIME FOR A CUP O' TEA.

WELL, ONE THING'S FOR SURE, MAW NEVER DOES ANYTHING BY HALF!

OH, BUT IT'S NO' ME THAT'S MAKIN' THE TEA!

HO-HO! THE BAIRN'S HOLDIN' A DOLLIES' TEA PARTY!

BAH! HALF-SIZED CUPS O' TEA NOW!

GROAN!

A punch on the nose, a broken arm—
Nae wonder Paw's filled with alarm!

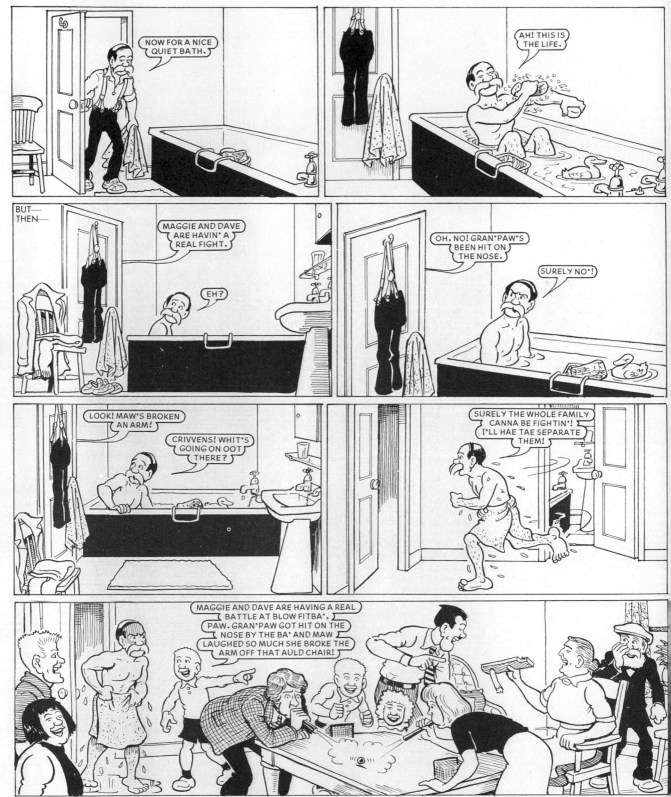

The lassies get a proper fright—

This "fortune teller's" always right!

They've hats big and small—

But Paw's caps them all!

You'll no' believe the Broons' new dish—

The family's eating " flying " fish!

It's a jumper, true—

And it's woolly, too!

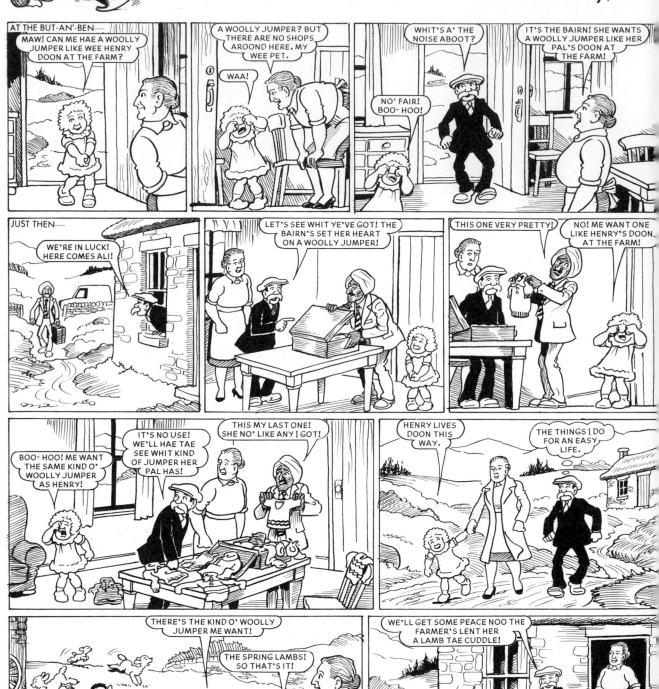

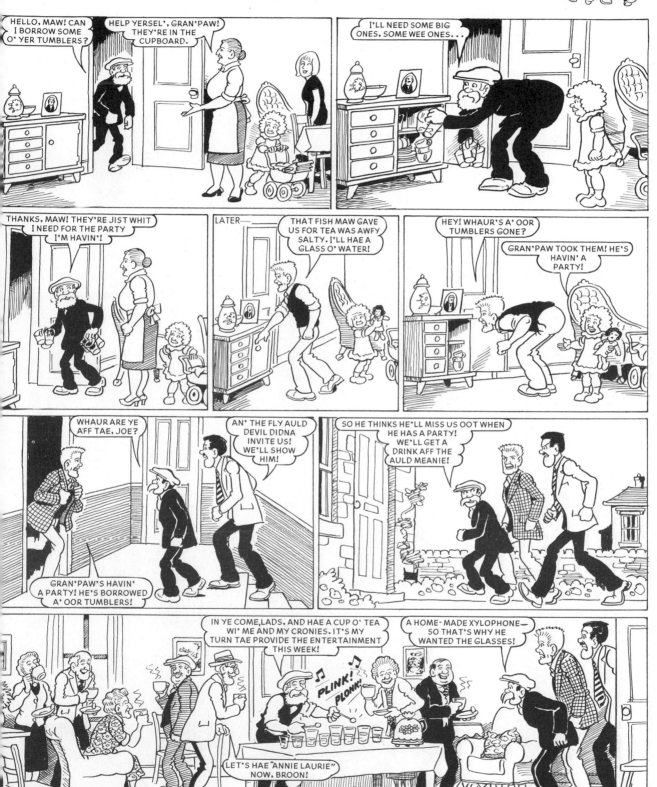

Watch this space—

For a funny race!

Laughs and shocks—

Wi' curly locks!

The Broons don't want another Gran—

They'll put a SPOKE in Gran'paw's plan!

A perfect match—

But there's a catch . . !

Inflation disna bother Paw—

Till the Bairn gives a mighty blaw!

Petrol's dear, but there's no stoppin'—

Paw Broon doing this bit o' shoppin'!

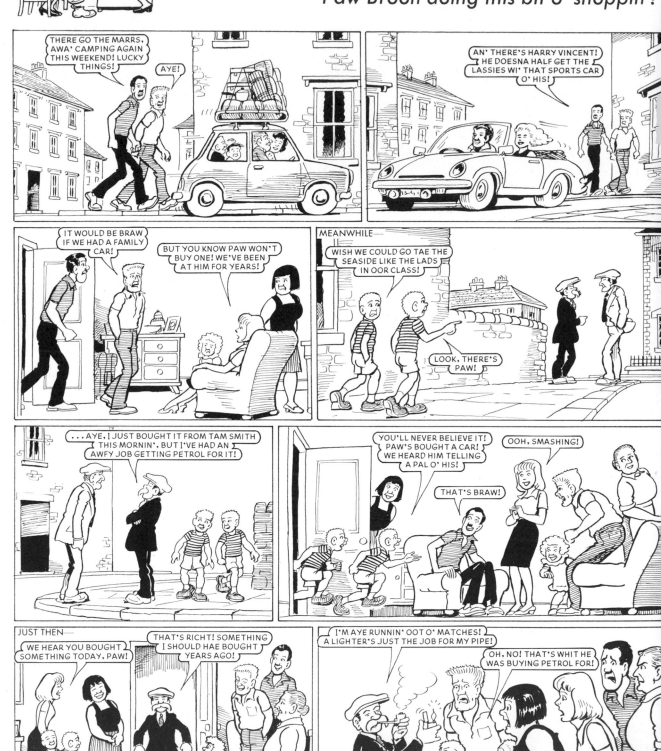

Jams galore—

And then some more!

AFTER WORK—
IT'S GOOD OF YOUR MAW TO INVITE ME FOR TEA, MAGGIE.

THERE'S AN EVEN WORSE JAM THAN USUAL, TONIGHT.

GLEBE STREET AT LAST. I THOUGHT WE'D NEVER GET THROUGH THAT TRAFFIC.
GLEBE ST.

OH, NO! THERE'S EVEN A JAM IN GLEBE STREET TONIGHT.
COAL MERCHANT

IN YOU COME, DAVE!

BAH! NOW THE DOOR'S JAMMED!

PHEW! I'VE HAD ENOUGH JAMS FOR ONE DAY. I'LL GO AND SAY HELLO TO MAW.

OH, HELLO, DAVE! I'LL BE MAKIN' THE TEA NEXT, AS SOON AS I'VE SEEN TAE THESE SKIMMINGS.

DID I HEAR SKIMMINGS?
I DIDNA KEN MAW WAS MAKIN' JAM.
OOH! I LOVE SKIMMINGS!

LET ME HAE FIRST TASTE, MAW!
I WANT SOME SKIMMINGS, MAW.
SAVE SOME FOR ME!
AND I THOUGHT I'D SEEN THE LAST OF JAMS!

Five o'clock on a Monday night—

That's the time for a funny sight!

Prince Charming and his " Cinderellie "—
Her foot's just perfect for that wellie!

The Broons buy lots o' doggy gear—
But there's something fishy going on here!

The lads are tired o' a' this liftin'—

But here's a thing they're grand at shiftin'!

There's no " ifs " and " buts "—
These lads are going " nuts!"

Where's the wettest place in toon—

When the rain comes pouring doon?

Gran'paw beams. It really looks—

As if he's in this girl's good books!

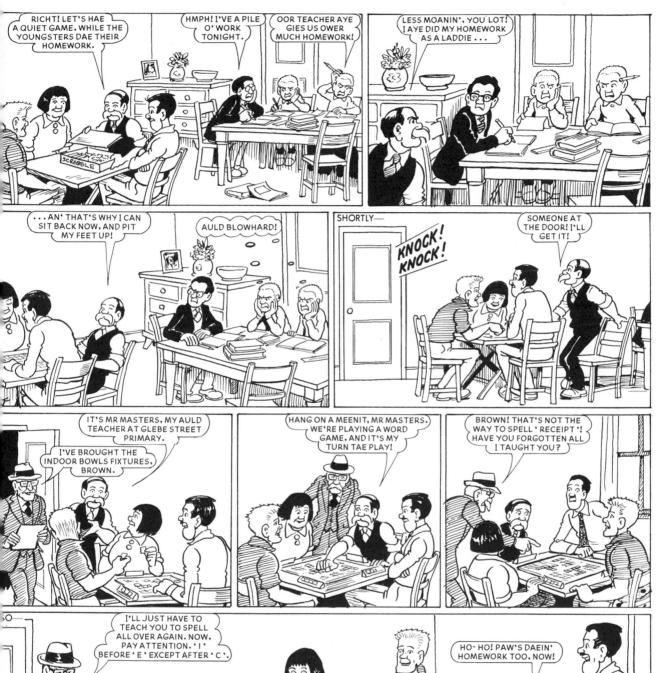

Watch the fitba'? No' a chance—

The womenfolk prefer romance!

Well, well, well, just feast your eyes—

On Maw Broon's perfect " bargain buys "!

The list poor Paw makes—

Is full of mistakes!

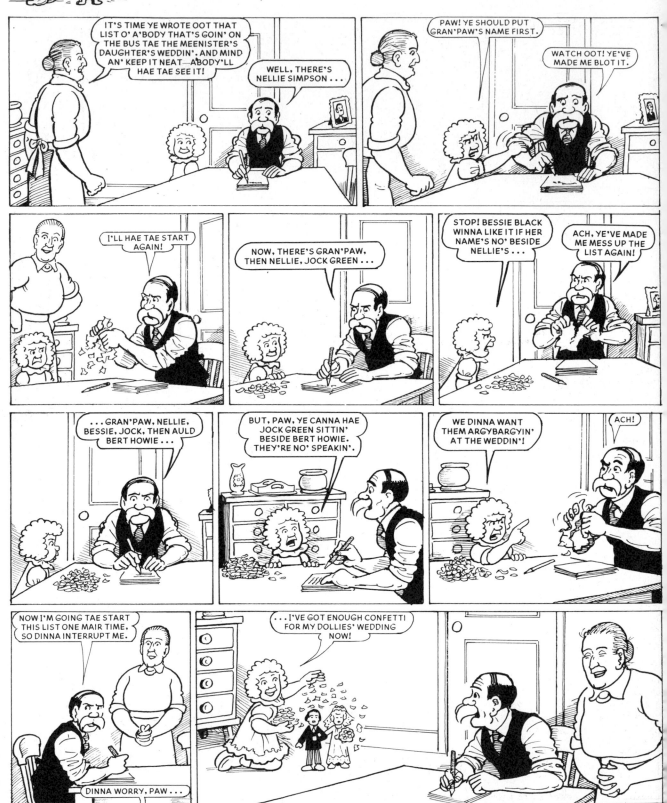

They dinna half fret—

Aboot Billy Greene's pet!

How to stay dry?—

Don't ask Mrs McKay!

Fancy breeks and shirt wi' flowers—

Nae wonder Maw Broon gasps and glowers!

THANKS FOR OFFERING TAE MAK' THE TEA AT THE YOUTH CLUB DANCE, PAW.

ANYTHING TAE HELP THE CLUB, HORACE! BUT I'M NO' GOING DOON THE ROAD WI' YOU DRESSED LIKE THAT. I'LL FOLLOW YE UP!

SHORTLY—

WELL, I'M OFF, MAW! WHIT THAE YOUNGSTERS NEED IS SOMEONE RESPECTABLE TAE LOOK UP TAE.

AT THE CLUB—

THANKS FOR COMIN' TAE HELP, MR BROON. WE WERE STUCK WHEN THE HALL-KEEPER WENT AFF SICK!

DINNA MENTION IT!

NOW, WHAUR ARE THE TEA-BAGS KEPT?

MAYBE THEY'RE UP HERE!

HEY! MR BROON . . . OOPS!

HELP!

JINGS! I'M SORRY! NEVER MIND, ANE O' THE GROUP HASNAE TURNED UP! HE'S ABOOT YOUR SIZE!

MEANWHILE—

. . . SUCH AN OBLIGING MAN, MR BROWN, AND SURE TO SET A GOOD EXAMPLE TO THE YOUNGSTERS.

SLAM!

SURELY THAT'S NO' HIM BACK ALREADY!

A GOOD EXAMPLE? OH, NO!

Dod boasts o' a' the things he's got—

But Paw just smiles. He has the lot!

It's a big " tea-hee "—

When they visit G.P.

Paw Broon wants some conversation—

But a' he gets is consternation!

Maw Broon proves she's crafty when—

She knocks " spots " off the domino men!

There are carpets galore—

And shocks in store!

Hen and Joe Broon pech and puff—

But guess which Broon is really tough

Fitba has its ups and doons—
When it's followed by the Broons!

. . . but things were just as bad—

When this auld chap was a lad!

Lots o' reek, lots o' puff—

Aye, that's really champion stuff!

Wi' shield and claymore aff they go—

A' set for battle wi' the foe!

Trust the twins—

Tae turn girns to grins!

The bunnet Gran'paw chooses—

Has some very special uses!

Paw can't remember that or this—

But he sure knows what day it is!

Hic-hic-hooray—

Paw saves Daph today!

" Lines " for Horace, just like a baddie?—
But there's never been a better laddie!

Peace an' quiet?—

It's mair like a riot!

Bingo or pictures, whit's it tae be?

Leave it tae Paw tae choose somethin' free!

Paw Broon gets an S.O.S.—

What's the trouble? Ye'll never guess!

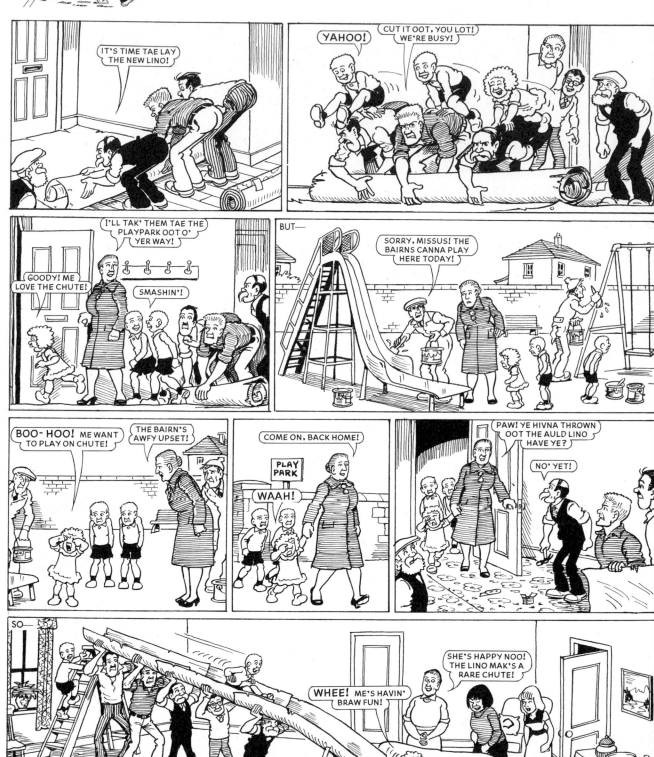

See the plan the Broon twins hatch—

Wi' a fill o' baccy and a match!

Gran'paw Broon has gone and done it—

A' because o' his big bunnet!

The sad tale o' a pie—

And a big black eye!

Help m' boab! Did ye ever see—
Such a fairy on a Christmas tree?

Their Christmas pud—

Is extra good!

When it's time tae celebrate New Year—

This " shortie " tak's the biscuit here!

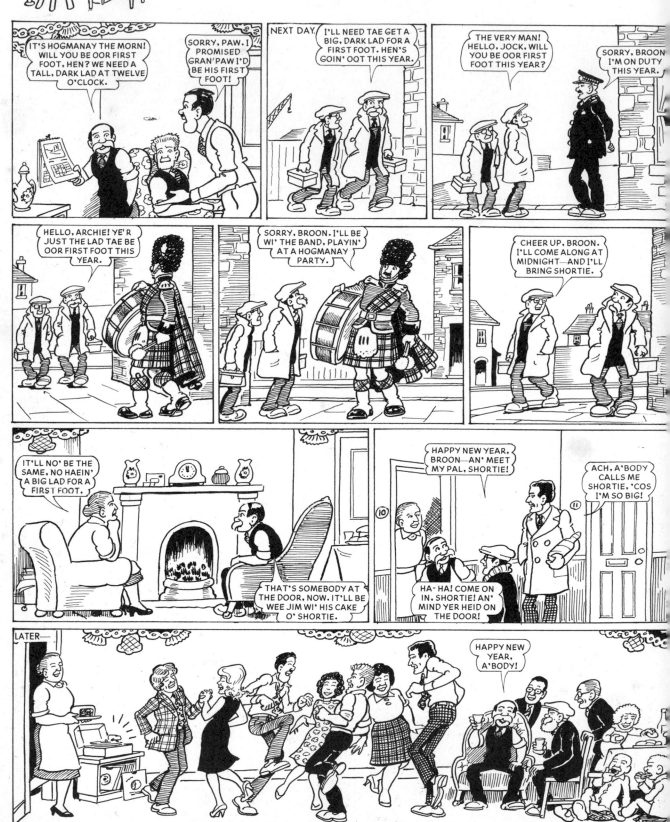